Wild About Wheels

RACING CARS

by Mari Schuh

raintree
a Capstone company — publishers for children

Raintree is an imprint of Capstone Global Library Limited, a company incorporated in England and Wales having its registered office at 264 Banbury Road, Oxford, OX2 7DY – Registered company number: 6695582

www.raintree.co.uk
myorders@raintree.co.uk

Text © Capstone Global Library Limited 2021
The moral rights of the proprietor have been asserted.

All rights reserved. No part of this publication may be reproduced in any form or by any means (including photocopying or storing it in any medium by electronic means and whether or not transiently or incidentally to some other use of this publication) without the written permission of the copyright owner, except in accordance with the provisions of the Copyright, Designs and Patents Act 1988 or under the terms of a licence issued by the Copyright Licensing Agency, 5th Floor, Shackleton House, 4 Battle Bridge Lane, London SE1 2HX (www.cla.co.uk). Applications for the copyright owner's written permission should be addressed to the publisher.

Edited by Carrie Sheely
Designed by Cynthia Della-Rovere
Original illustrations © Capstone Global Library Limited 2021
Picture research by Eric Gohl
Production by Katy LaVigne
Originated by Capstone Global Library Ltd

978 1 3982 0383 9 (hardback)
978 1 3982 0382 2 (paperback)

British Library Cataloguing in Publication Data
A full catalogue record for this book is available from the British Library.

Acknowledgements
We would like to thank the following for permission to reproduce photographs: Associated Press: Reinhold Matay, 10; Capstone Studio: Karon Dubke, 21; Dreamstime: Walter Arce, 9; Newscom: Cal Sport Media/Russell Hons, 4, Icon SMI/David Allio, 15; Shutterstock: action sports, 6, 14, Action Sports Photography, 5, 7, 18, Admad Faizal Yahya, 13, HodagMedia, 16, Jens Mommens, cover, back cover, John J. Klaiber Jr, 12, Mladen Pavlovic, 8, Natursports, 17, 19, Phillip Rubino, 11, StevanZZ, background (racing track)

Every effort has been made to contact copyright holders of material reproduced in this book. Any omissions will be rectified in subsequent printings if notice is given to the publisher.

All the internet addresses (URLs) given in this book were valid at the time of going to press. However, due to the dynamic nature of the internet, some addresses may have changed, or sites may have changed or ceased to exist since publication. While the author and publisher regret any inconvenience this may cause readers, no responsibility for any such changes can be accepted by either the author or the publisher.

Printed and bound in the United Kingdom.

Contents

What racing cars do 4
Look inside 8
Look outside 12

Racing car diagrams 18
Design your own racing car . . . 20
Glossary 22
Find out more 23
Index 24

Words in **bold** are in the glossary.

What racing cars do

Vroom! Racing cars zoom around the track. They come around the curve and zip towards the finish line. Which one will win?

Racing cars are built for speed. Most races are held at special tracks. Other cars race on dirt tracks. All the races are fast.

CHEVROLET
Sprint
CUP SERIES
KENSETH
DOLLAR GENERAL
CAMRY
NEWMAN
GORDON
JOHNSON

stock car

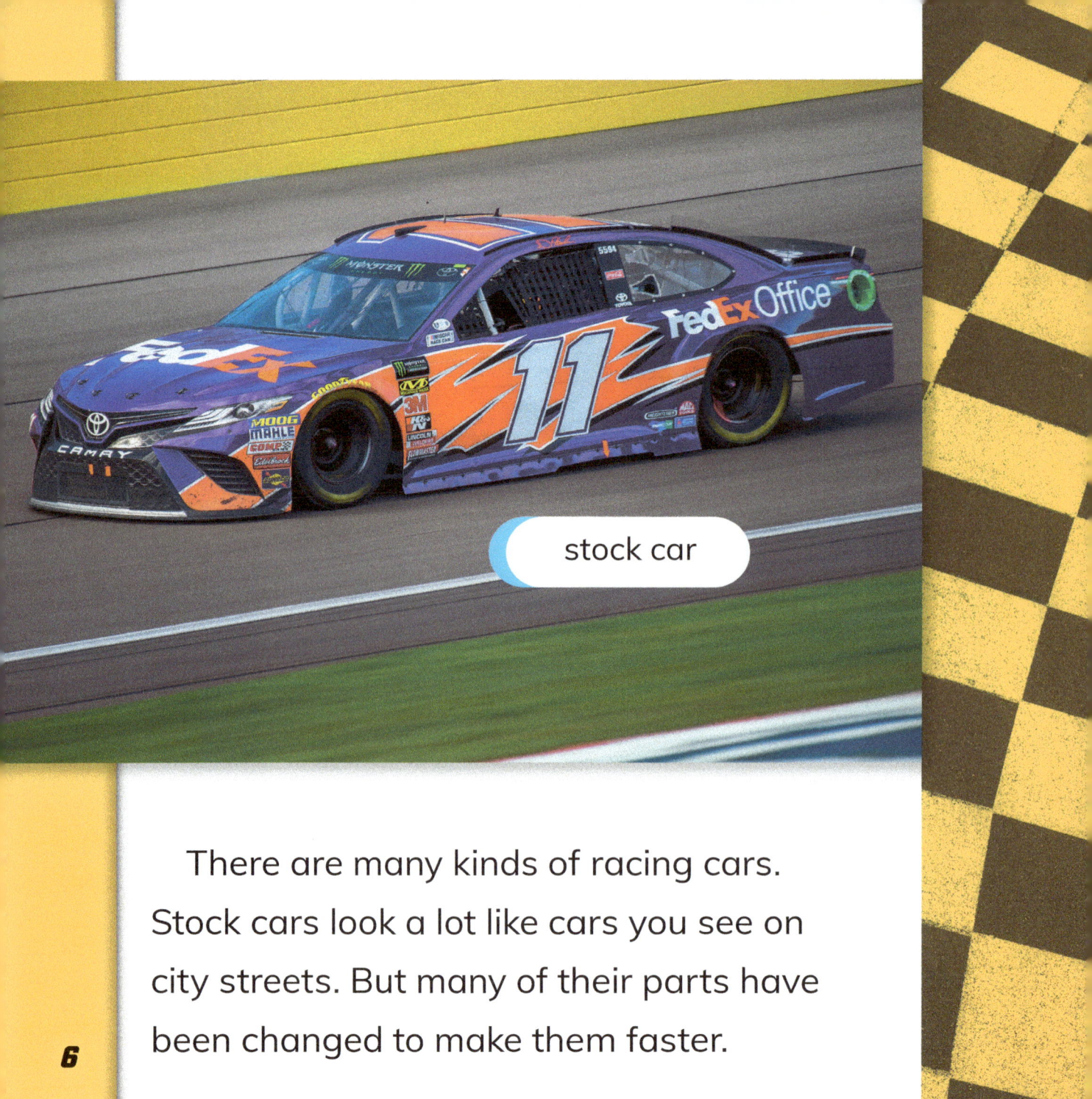

There are many kinds of racing cars. Stock cars look a lot like cars you see on city streets. But many of their parts have been changed to make them faster.

Some racing cars have open wheels. That means the wheels are not covered. The **cockpit** is open too. The driver's head sticks out. Formula 1 (F1) cars and IndyCars have open wheels.

IndyCar

Look inside

Look inside the cockpit! A **harness** keeps the driver in place. The driver turns the car with the steering wheel. It often has many switches, knobs and dials. Some change the way the car balances round corners. Others send messages to the driver's crew.

F1 car steering wheel

harness

stock car engine

Racing cars have big **engines**. The engines can be in the car's front or back. They give racing cars power to reach high speeds. Top fuel **dragsters** can go more than 480 kilometres (300 miles) per hour!

Racing car engines work very hard. They often do not last long. Teams may need to replace them many times in a racing season.

top fuel dragster

11

Look outside

Normal car tyres have bumps or **grooves** called tread. Racing cars use tyres like this in wet weather.

tyre with tread

When it is dry, racing cars are often fitted with smooth tyres called slicks. During a race, the tyres get hot. They get sticky. They grip the dry track. Slicks wear out quickly. Many tyres are used in one race.

slick

Racing cars are colourful. They are covered in stickers called **decals**. NASCAR racing cars are particularly colourful. They often have a big number on the sides. This helps fans see their favourite cars. It's easier to see them as they speed round the track.

LES
OLSON
COMPANY
SHARP COPIERS
SWINDELL
DIRECTV
CHEVY
ARMORALL
MAXIM

Racing cars have lots of parts to help drivers. Many racing cars have **wings** or **spoilers**. These parts help push air down. This helps the tyres grip the track. The car can go faster while turning.

rear wing

front wing

Some cars have a window net. It helps keep drivers safe. During a crash, it keeps the driver's arms inside the car.

Racing car diagrams

stock car

window net

spoiler

slicks

18

F1 car

- rear wing
- cockpit
- slicks
- front wing

19

Design your own racing car

If you could design your own racing car, what would it look like? Would it look much like a normal car? Would the driver sit inside the car's body? Or would the car have an open cockpit? Would the tyres be covered or uncovered? What colour would the car's body be? Draw a picture of your racing car.

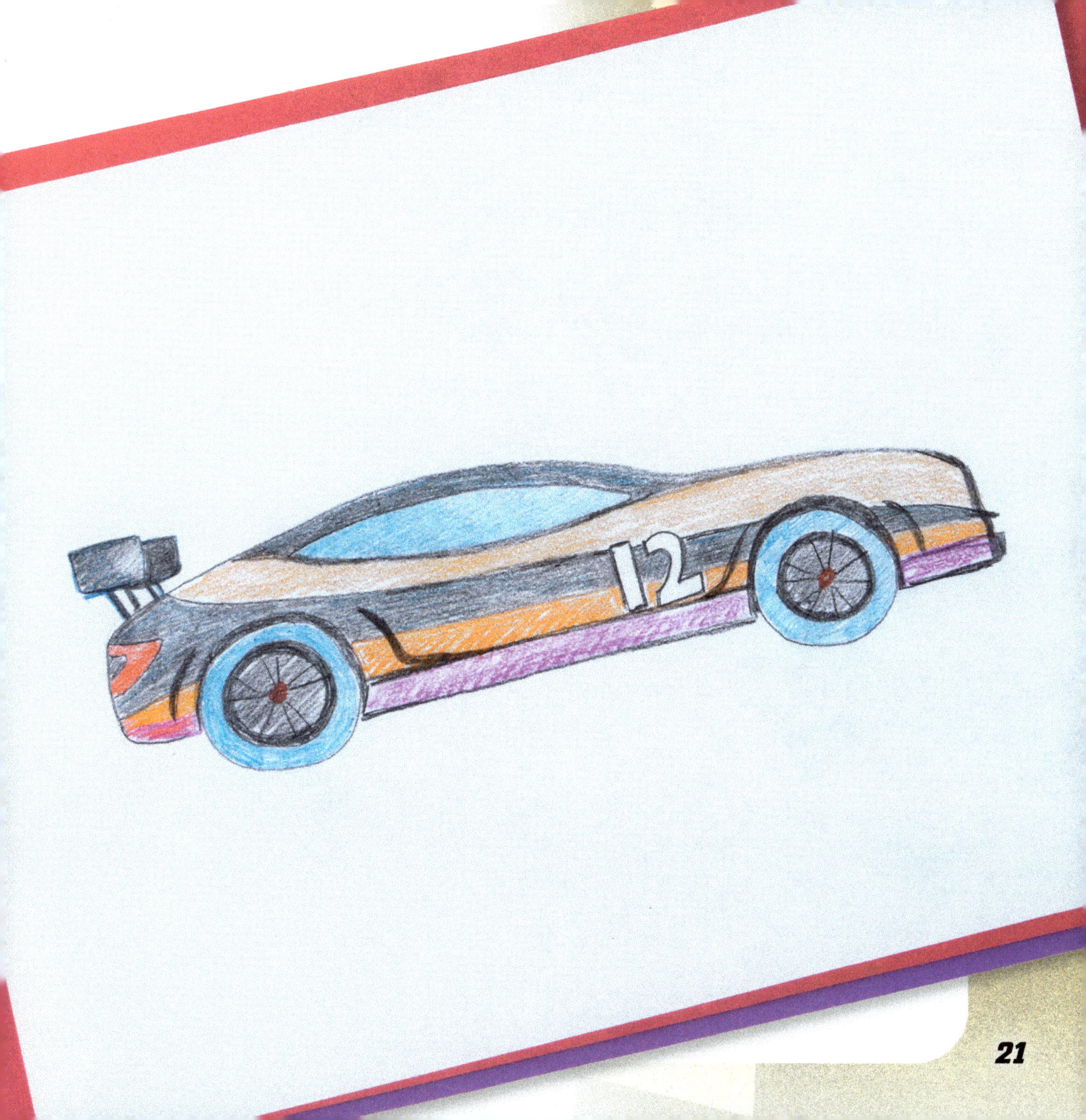
12

Glossary

cockpit place where a driver sits in a racing car

decal picture or label that can be stuck to hard surfaces, such as the shell of a racing car

dragster type of car built to race for a short distance in a straight line against another car

engine machine that uses fuel to power a vehicle

groove long cut in something

harness set of straps used to help keep a racing car driver safe

spoiler wing-like device attached to the back of a racing car

wing long, flat panel on the front or back of some racing cars

Find out more

Books

Formula 1 Driver - Lewis Hamilton vs Nico Rosberg (The Inside Track), Paul Mason (Franklin Watts, 2016)

Indy Cars (Full Throttle), Thomas K. Adamson (Epic, 2019)

Ultimate Cars: The World's Most Amazing Speed Machines, Clive Gifford (Carlton Kids, 2018)

Website

www.dkfindout.com/uk/transport/history-cars/racing-cars/
Find out about the history of racing cars.

Index

cockpit 7, 8

crew 8

decals 14

engine 10–11

Formula 1 cars 7

harness 8

IndyCars 7

NASCAR 14

slicks 12

spoilers 16

steering wheel 8

stock car 6

top fuel dragster 10

track 4, 12, 14, 16

tyres 12, 16

wheels 7

window net 17

wings 16